Father Browne's
SHIPS & SHIPPING
Images from the renowned photographer of *Titanic*

American ladies disembarking from the tender America *(from* Father Browne's *Titanic* Album)

Father Browne's
SHIPS & SHIPPING

Images from the renowned photographer of *Titanic*

E.E. O'DONNELL SJ

WOLFHOUND PRESS

First published in 2000 by
WOLFHOUND PRESS
68 Mountjoy Square, Dublin 1

ISBN 0 86327 758 6

Book layout and cover design by Ted & Ursula O'Brien, Dublin
Typeset by ArtLine Limited, Dublin
Duotone separations by Colour Repro Limited, Dublin
Printed and bound in Belgium by Proost N.V.

Photographic prints by Davison & Associates, Dublin
(contact address for prints: 69b Heather Road, Sandyford Ind. Estate, Dublin 18)

British Library Cataloguing in Publication data: a catalogue record for this book is available in the British Library.

Profits made by the Jesuit Order from the sale of Father Browne's books and prints go to the Jesuit Solidarity Fund.

5 4 3 2 1

Cover Photographs: Front: *'Shooting the Sun': crewmen employing a sextant aboard SS* Port Melbourne *in the South Atlantic Ocean (1924).*
Back: *In Alexandra Basin, Dublin, (1932).*

ALSO PUBLISHED by WOLFHOUND PRESS, DUBLIN
The Annals of Dublin (1987)
Father Browne's Ireland (1988)
The Genius of Father Browne (1989)
Father Browne's Dublin (1990)
Father Browne's Cork (1992)
Father Browne: A Life in Pictures (1994)
Father Browne's Australia (1995, 1999)
Father Browne's England (1996)
Images of Aran (1997)
Father Browne's *Titanic* Album (1997)

PUBLISHED by THE SOCIETY OF IRISH FORESTERS
Forest Images: Father Browne's Woodland Photographs (1993)

PUBLISHED by ANATOLIA EDITIONS, PARIS
L'Irlande du père Browne (1996) – Available from the author

CONTENTS

Father Browne with some of the officers of the SS Port Melbourne *at Cape Town (1924)*

Father Frank Browne: Photographer

'There is however a deeper element within these pictures. Their skilful structure and timing capture something of the experience of the moment, the pictures grip the imagination and convey atmosphere and mood and communicate feelings both pleasing and sometimes questioning. The viewer is challenged to engage in thought, to seek further meaning; surely at this point we are confronted with truly artistically expressive material. It is this artistic achievement that places Father Browne in the company of great photographers of the 20th century. Others have recorded the quaint and historic in Irish life but Father Browne has captured the experience of a half century in the life of this country.'

David Davison, quoted in: *Father Browne: A Life in Pictures* (Wolfhound, 1994).

'Father Browne of the *Titanic'* is how many people depict the Jesuit priest whose photographs of ships are represented here. This, in some ways, is strange since there are only about eighty photographs of that unfortunate liner in Father Browne's Collection of 42,000 pictures. Moreover, photography was of secondary interest to a priest who had dedicated his life to the service of the Gospel.

Up to about 1950 Father Browne's name was a household one in Ireland and in photographic circles worldwide. By the time of his death in 1960, at the age of eighty, that name had begun to fade from public consciousness. Most of his contemporaries in the Jesuit Order were already dead and many of his younger confrères were unaware of his past glory. His trunk full of negatives, all neatly captioned and dated, was consigned to the Jesuit Province Archives where it lay unopened for a quarter of a century.

Father Browne's story does not end with his death. His posthumous fame continues to grow. Praise from the critics is mounting all the time and there is a constant demand for more information about the man behind the camera.

Francis Mary Hegarty Browne, the youngest of eight children, was born in the Sunday's Well suburb of Cork city in the south of Ireland in 1880. He came from a well-to-do family who lived in a substantial house on Buxton Hill. His mother, *née* Brigid Hegarty, was a daughter of the Lord Mayor of Cork, James Hegarty, a prominent personality in local politics for decades. His father was a prominent industrialist.

Both of Frank's parents were highly religious so it is hardly surprising that one daughter became a nun and two sons became priests. Both parents died while Frank was young, so it was his uncle, Robert Browne, Bishop of Cloyne, who was responsible for his early education at the Bower Convent, Athlone, and Belvedere College, Dublin.

Gregarious by nature, Frank took an active part in school field games and was an automatic choice for the First XV in rugby. His secondary education was completed with a Grand Tour of Europe in 1897. Equipped with a Kodak camera for the first time, he travelled with his brother William through France, Italy, Switzerland and Germany. These first photographs, taken at the age of seventeen, already show signs of the expertise that was to follow. Despite the relatively primitive photographic equipment of the age, and despite the slowness of shutter speeds, Frank had an intuitive grasp of composition, a talent that was to be fostered later on when he studied Italian art in some depth.

On his return to Ireland he joined the Jesuits. For the three years from the autumn of 1899, 'Mister' Frank Browne was a student of the Royal University of Ireland, Dublin. Another Old Belvederian, James Joyce, was a strict contemporary for these three university years and 'Mr Browne, the Jesuit' features (favourably!) in the pages of *Finnegans Wake*.

He was then sent to study philosophy for three years at Chieri in Northern Italy. At the end of that third year at Chieri there was an extremely formidable examination, called the 'Centone', open to the public and, although the entire proceeding was in Latin, many of the intelligentsia of Turin would attend. Frank passed with flying colours. He then returned to spend five years teaching at Belvedere College, Dublin.

During the first of his five years as a teacher, he founded *The Belvederian*, the Camera Club and the Cycling Club. The Camera Club, which (like the college annual) is still going strong, taught boys the elements of photography and provided dark-room facilities.

In 1911 he began the penultimate stage of his Jesuit training, studying theology for four years, being ordained priest after the third of these. All was plain sailing until suddenly, on 3 April, 1912, he received a letter that would change the course of his life. The letter came from the White Star Line and it contained a first-class ticket, a gift from his Uncle Robert, for the first two legs of the maiden voyage of the *Titanic*.

The morning of Wednesday 10 April, 1912, found him on the platform of Waterloo Station in London, ready to board 'the first and last *Titanic Special*'. He had his camera with him, and of course was fortunate to disembark at Cobh (then Queenstown) in Ireland. Four days later the great tragedy occurred and Frank Browne's photographs illustrated newspaper reports around the world telling of the sinking of the *Titanic*. For lack of space here, I must refer readers to my book, *Father Browne's Titanic Album*, for the full story and the extraordinary images of the great liner.

He was ordained to the priesthood in 1915. Early in 1916 he responded to an appeal for army chaplains from the Chief Chaplain to the Forces, London. Father Browne joined the First Battalion of the Irish Guards and was to serve in the front line in France and Flanders right up to the end of the war in November 1918. Injured five times – he had to have his whole jaw wired up on one occasion – and gassed once, he won the Military Cross and Bar and the *Croix de Guerre* from both France and Belgium. He was also described by his commanding officer, Colonel (later Field-Marshal Earl) Alexander, as 'the bravest man I ever met'.

The *Irish Guards Association Journal* of February 1961 carried an obituary notice on Father Browne, in which Lord Nugent wrote: 'Everyone in the Battalion, officer or man, Catholic or Protestant, loved and respected Father Browne and he had great influence for good. He was a brave man in the true sense for he was conscious of danger but never allowed shells or bullets, which he hated as much as any of us, to divert him from his duty. Where the wounded or dying lay, there Father Browne was to be found to give them comfort and peace... A great Christian, a brave and lovable man, we who knew him so well will always be grateful for his friendship and for the example that he set.'

And of course, he had his camera with him in the trenches, leaving us with some powerful war photographs.

In 1920 Father Browne was forty years of age and had been in the Jesuit Order for twenty-three of those years. But he had still to complete his Jesuit training. The final stage of his formation, called 'tertianship', was normally done immediately after theology. In his case it was deferred for the four years he was with the Irish Guards. This entailed a return to the novitiate; but one difference between tertianship and novicehood was that he was allowed to keep his camera!

No record remains of Father Browne's stance during the Anglo-Irish War or the Civil War. Among the few photographs taken during these troubled years was a series showing his native Cork after it had been destroyed by the 'Black and Tans' (British auxiliary security forces) in December 1920.

In February 1921, he took his Final Vows as a Jesuit. In 1922 he was appointed Superior of St Francis Xavier's Church on Gardiner Street, Dublin. The saying among Jesuits at the time was that it was 'more important to be a Gardiner Street Father than a rural Rector' – so this was a major promotion.

Here, he carried out many practical improvements, but his health began to deteriorate. His doctor recommended dry air and a warmer climate. He sailed for Australia on 12 March 1924, leaving Falmouth on board the liner *Port Melbourne*. He stopped over for some weeks in Cape Town, then went on to Australia on the *Arundel Castle*. Browne took dozens of pictures during the voyage, as evidenced here in this volume. During his stay in Australia he took over a thousand pictures before the end of 1925, travelling over three thousand miles in the outback (See *Father Browne's Australia*, 1995).

The return journey to Ireland began with a voyage on the *Orama* from Perth to Ceylon, now Sri Lanka, via the Cocos Islands. From Ceylon he travelled via Somaliland and Yemen to Aden. Then, past Ethiopia, Sudan and Saudi Arabia, his ship sailed on through the Red Sea to Suez. Passing through that canal, he photographed life in Egypt on both the African and Asian banks before arriving in Port Said.

From Port Said he sailed across the Mediterranean Sea, first to Salonika in Greece and then, past Mount Etna on Sicily, to Naples. A three-day stopover there gave him the opportunity to visit Pompeii and photograph its extraordinary remains.

His next ship took him to Toulon in the south of France with its Napoleonic forts guarding the harbour; then to Gibraltar where again he stayed for three days. He took some fine pictures of the Rock itself and then crossed into Spain to visit Algeciras and La Linea.

From Gibraltar he voyaged to Lisbon, which brought back memories of his 1909 visit, and from the Portuguese capital it was non-stop to Plymouth with a rough passage through the Bay of Biscay. After a short stay in England, Father Browne returned to his post at Gardiner Street. With his lungs cured, permanently as it turned out, his fame as a preacher increased: people would come from distant parts to hear his sermons. His pastoral duties were central to his life.

It was in 1925 that he began to photograph Dublin city extensively, taking nearly five thousand pictures of the capital, the final roll of film being shot in 1957. There are nearly 42,000 negatives in his Collection altogether, 36,000 (approximately) taken in Ireland. By December of 1925 he had taken less than four thousand photographs, a quarter of these in Australia, the bulk of his foreign shipping photographs. In other words, the greater part of his photographic work was still to come. He took lessons as a pilot in 1926, again with photography in mind.

By 1927 Father Browne was a member of the Photographic Society of Ireland and of the Dublin Camera Club. Being a Corkman, and one who often returned to his native county, he exhibited his work at the Cork Camera Club's annual exhibition. He won prizes there too, an early example being 'Georgian Splendour', which won him a medal in 1928. All this time Father Browne's reputation as a preacher in Gardiner Street continued to grow; so much so that his next assignment was to the Mission and Retreat Staff of the Irish Jesuits, a post he would occupy for the next thirty years.

When Father Browne arrived in Emo in 1928, the community was a tightly knit unit, so the new 'Missioner' must have felt something of an outsider. 'Missioner' was the name given to the group of eleven or twelve Irish Jesuits whose work was to give parish missions throughout Ireland and Britain and to give enclosed retreats to priests, nuns, working men and schoolchildren. By all accounts, he shunned the 'fire and brimstone' style of preaching. During 1929 he began the routine that he was to follow for so many years, travelling continually from parish to parish, mainly by train, throughout Ireland.

During the 1932 Eucharistic Congress in Dublin, from a rooftop vantage point he was able to capture in still and moving images the impressive scene as O'Connell Street began to fill with people arriving *en masse* for the final benediction of the Congress. After the celebrations had come to a conclusion, he returned to Emo and developed his films. (For years the rest of the community would be complaining about lack of access to the bathroom, which not only stank of chemicals but had the bath full of Browne films undergoing a final wash.) He then did quite an expert montage job on his first 16mm movie, entitled *The Eucharistic Congress of 1932*. He had the occasional captions for the silent motion picture printed decoratively by Kodak & Co. in Harrow, England. This film is still extant, a copy preserved by the Irish Film Archives.

In subsequent years he made quite a few other 16mm motion pictures. The best known of these was his history of the Foxford Woollen Mills in County Mayo, made in the 1930s. Most of his other films were commissioned by a variety of governmental or educational bodies, including films on Forestry Work, on the Garda Síochána for the Commissioner of Police, on Irish Creameries, and on the rural electrification of Ireland.

Between 1933 and the outbreak of World War II in 1939 Father Browne spent a good proportion of his life in parishes in Wales and Scotland – including the islands of Jura and Islay – but it was in England that he found himself most frequently. During the summer of 1933 he paid a visit to the Kodak Works at Harrow, near London, where he was able to photograph cameras being manufactured and where he had an important interview with the Managing Director, George Davison. Davison had been a prominent artistic photographer and a founder of a secessionist movement called The Linked Ring, in 1892. This group founded the London Salon of Photography, and it is interesting to note that Father Browne was instrumental in the foundation of the Irish Salon, with similar aims to those of The Ring. The Ring eventually recombined with the Royal Photographic Society in 1910. Clearly Father Browne had found a kindred spirit in photography and, presumably in consequence of this, George Davison arranged for him to receive a free supply of film for life. By way of return, he made regular contributions to *The Kodak Magazine*. Many of these features were on the cathedrals of England. While in London the British Museum commissioned him to photograph certain antiquities of England. He gave a lot of time to this important work and afterwards, when he had returned to Ireland, continued a lengthy correspondence with the Museum.

The years 1939 to 1945 in the Republic of Ireland were euphemistically called 'the Emergency', the Republic being neutral during World War II. When the war broke out in 1939 the former military chaplain and hero of the Great War was fifty-nine years of age. Nonetheless, he was quick to volunteer his services and was accepted. However, he was refused permission to go by his Jesuit superior.

He continued his photographic work during the Emergency years. He made many nature studies – the life cycle of a swan; 'Trees', 'Seasons', 'Clouds', 'Flowers' and 'Animals'. Most of these nature photographs were taken with the new camera, a Contax 'Number Two' which he had been given by his brother-in-law in 1937. Photographers will also be intrigued to learn that Father Browne manufactured his own 'portable dark-room' in which he could change films in the open air.

Also during the Emergency, Father Browne continued to experiment with colour photography. We know that he had worked with 'DufayColor' in the middle of the 1930s but no example of this work remains in his Collection. His early colour photographs, however, still exist and have been purchased at specialist auctions as late as the 1990s. It was not until the early 1950s that he began to make consistent use of Kodak Safety Film. (Over three-quarters of his Collection – i.e. some 30,000 photographs – is therefore on the older nitrate stock.) It was also in the early 1950s that he acquired his last camera, a compact Leica.

Now in his seventies, he was still giving parish missions throughout Ireland. He also found time to become a more active member of the Irish Photographic Society. He went on many field expeditions with this Society and adjudicated its photographic competitions. By way of practising what he was preaching about the photography of buildings, he made a point of recording on film the Great Houses of Ireland and their owners.

Travel and all forms of transport were subjects dear to Father Browne's heart – including, of course, ships. As a youth and as a young man he had taken the tenders from Queenstown (Cobh) to photograph the transatlantic liners; he recorded all the ships on which he had travelled himself, including the liners to and from Australia as well as the mailboat between Dún Laoghaire and Holyhead and the B&I ferry between Dublin and Liverpool; he photographed yacht-races in Cork Harbour, Sydney Harbour and Dublin Bay; in fact he snapped anything that floated, from the powerful tug at the Albert Dock in London to the humble barge on the Grand Canal in Dublin, not forgetting the trawlers at Clogherhead, Killybegs and Balbriggan.

Trains were another passion. His Collection contains well over a thousand photographs of trains, taken not only in England and Ireland but in Australia, Egypt, Italy and France. His pictures of Irish trains are alphabetised neatly and show not only locomotives and rolling-stock but also the railway-men at work. Like most railway lovers, he must have lamented the passing of the steam age. Nevertheless he enjoyed at least two journeys when he was allowed to handle the controls of the new-fangled diesel locomotives.

As regards road transport, the Browne Collection has pictures of everything from trams to donkey-tandems, from bicycles to articulated lorries, from horses-and-carts to traction engines. As one works chronologically through the photographs, the horse-drawn phaetons and landaus give way to the earliest 'Tin Lizzies' and the beautiful early Benz.

In the middle of the 1950s his services were requested by the parish priest of Beechwood Avenue Church in Dublin. He concluded his sermon there one evening by saying: 'Now if there are any young men, or even any not-so-young men, listening to me tonight who feel they could replace me in the Jesuit Order (because I haven't much longer to live), let them come in and have a word with me after-wards in the sacristy.' One 'not-so-young man' – a thirty-two-year-old – was listening and did go to the sacristy to speak with Father Browne after the ceremony. Paddy Doyle joined the Jesuits and later became the Provincial Superior of the Order in Ireland.

Such was the influence of Father Browne in the pulpit. But he was correct in thinking that his preaching days were nearly finished. Increasing infirmity curtailed his movements and he did most of his work in Dublin. He was beginning to show his years, as can be seen in a photograph taken by a friend (Graham Urch) in Brown's pharmacy on St Stephen's Green in Dublin. During the last three years of his life, Father Browne contributed to many newspapers and magazines in Ireland and England.

Over the years, he sent all his photographic earnings to the Provincial Treasurer of the Jesuits, keeping a meticulous tally of the amount he had forwarded. At his own suggestion, these funds went to the formation of what he delightfully called 'Brownie Burses' for the education of Jesuit students. All told, he sent over a thousand pounds to these burses between 1937 and 1959 – a lot of money in those days.

During 1958 and 1959 Father Browne put the finishing touches to the catalogue of his Collection. Before computers, this was quite a task. He listed separately the different countries where he had worked and then made sub-sections for Archaeological Remains, Abbeys, Castles, Colleges, Convents and so on.

The most important part of his catalogue is the alphabetical list of the people he had photographed during his sixty years behind the camera. The vast majority were ordinary men and women, including ordinary Jesuits, though the list also includes some prominent names: politicians such as William Cosgrave, Éamon de Valéra and Tim Healy; prelates such as Cardinals Bourne, Logue and McRory; ambassadors such as Marchese Giovanni Sali of Italy and Mgr Paschal Robinson of the Vatican; writers such as G.K.Chesterton, Rudyard Kipling and Sir Shane Leslie; members of titled families such as Lords Bective, Castlerosse, Dunsany and Rosse.

During 1959 Father Browne's health deteriorated and he was hospitalised twice. His last photo-graphs were taken at Milltown Park where he focused on the neighbouring Jesuit establishments: Gonzaga College and the then Catholic Workers College, now the National College of Ireland. His very last pictures were of the grounds of Milltown Park itself, taken in colour.

In the summer of 1960 Father Browne was told that he was dying. Faithful to the last, Lord Alexander travelled from England to visit him on his deathbed. He died on 7 July. Among the many obituary notices, *The Province News* had a paragraph that can be quoted by way of summation:

> Father Browne was a most priestly man. This priestliness he carried into the pulpit. He was never cheap or frivolous. His preaching was always impressive, his words well chosen, his examples apt. He had a very friendly and sympathetic approach to his congregation. His confessional was always crowded and never hurried. There was the kindly word for every-one. With the secular clergy he was extremely popular, yet always reserved and dignified. It is the truth that he never forgot that he was a priest and a Jesuit.

Father Browne's funeral took place on 9 July, 1960. Given that he took nearly 42,000 photographs his life, it is no surprise that one of these was of the Jesuit burial-plot in Glasnevin Cemetery, Dublin, where he now rests in peace.

When he died very few people were aware that he had taken nearly 42,000 pictures between 1897 and 1957. These negatives, all neatly captioned and dated, were stored in a trunk in the corner of his room in Milltown. After his death the trunk was deposited in the Jesuit Province Archives in the basement of the Provincial's house. There it lay unopened for the next twenty-six years. I had the privilege of unearthing this treasure trove in 1986.

While working at the Provincial's house, I had often seen that trunk lying in the bottom of a press, buried under a few feet of documents. One day, I decided to see what it contained. When I had extricated the trunk, I saw that it bore the legend, in chalked letters: 'Father Browne's Photographs'. Intrigued, I opened the lid. Packs and packs of negatives lay before me. The first one I looked at was captioned 'Pompeii, 1925'.

An expert on the restoration of old photographs, David Davison confirmed that the early negatives were already disintegrating and that the durability of nitrate film was running out fast. He also told me, to my horror, the financial cost of saving the Collection. It was at this point that the London *Independent* published a full-page feature on Father Browne and his photography. Written by Alan Murdock and Brian Harris (who went on to win the Photographer of the Year award), it stressed the necessity of saving the Collection by putting it on safety-film. Armed with this material, I approached Allied Irish Banks to seek sponsorship for the salvage operation. The response, to the bank's eternal credit, was a favourable one. For the next three years, David Davison and his son Edwin toiled away at saving the negatives and recording the captions on a database system. They managed to save even the oldest negatives before the images disappeared. The Collection is now saved and cross-referenced, thanks to their efforts.

Over a dozen books of Browne photographs have now been published and there are many more in the pipeline. Exhibitions of his work have been shown all over Ireland by Ark Life Assurance, a subsidiary of Allied Irish Banks. Exhibitions outside Ireland have taken place at Paris, Montpellier and Lorient in France, at Frankfurt in Germany, at Braja in Portugal and at eight venues in Japan courtesy of Sony. Another major exhibition will tour America, in the near future. Television documentaries have been aired by Radio Telefís Éireann and there are plans afoot to film his *Titanic* story.

At the Georges Pompidou Centre in Paris, the French Minister for Culture likened Father Browne's work to that of the French genius Cartier-Bresson. What higher compliment can one get?

E.E. O'Donnell SJ

1

FATHER BROWNE'S ALBUM FACSIMILES

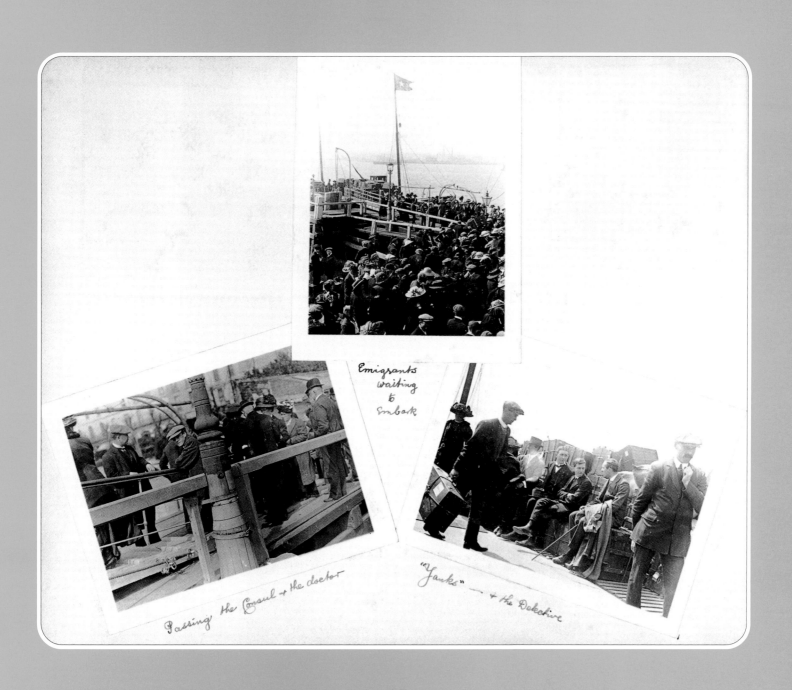

Emigrants waiting to Embark

Passing the Consul + the doctor

"Yanks" — + the Detective

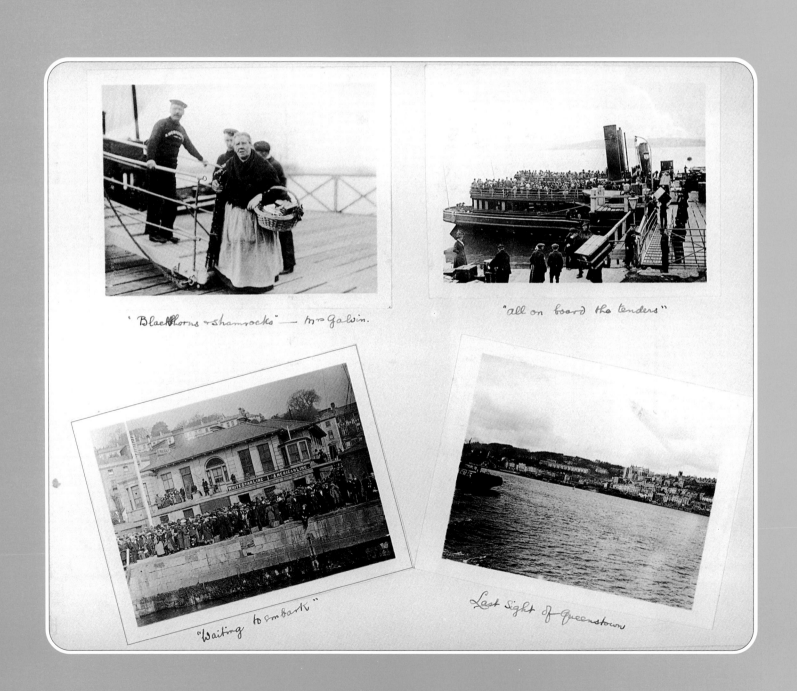

"Blackthorns & shamrocks" — Mrs Galvin.

"all on board the tenders"

"Waiting to embark"

Last sight of Queenstown

"In the Offing". Mauretania

Length   790 feet
Breadth   88 feet
Draught (fully loaded) 37½ feet
Depth (Keel-Boat deck)   80 feet
Tonnage   32,000 tons
Height to top of Funnels 153 ft
    "   "   " Masts   216 ft

"At anchor" - Mauretania

Horsepower   68,000
Speed   25·5 knots.
Watertight Compartments 157.
Passengers { 1st   550
            { and   550
            { 3rd 1300
Crew   850.

"The gangway of the Mauretania"
Transferring Mails

"An unusual transfer"
Tenders changing passengers
and
baggage in mid-channel.

"Emigrants' farewell"

The occasion of this transfer was the arrival from Lpool by the "Baltic" of some passengers, who had missed the slower "Haverford", & who had been permitted to travel to Queenstown by the Baltic. The Baltic left Lpool two hours after the Haverford & arrived in Queenstown 1½ hrs before her. The tender "Ireland" was returning from the Baltic & meeting the "America", bound towost the Haverford the passengers & luggage were transferred in the channel.

Calm waters
near the Harbour's
mouth. Liner (Celtic)
approaching in the
distance.

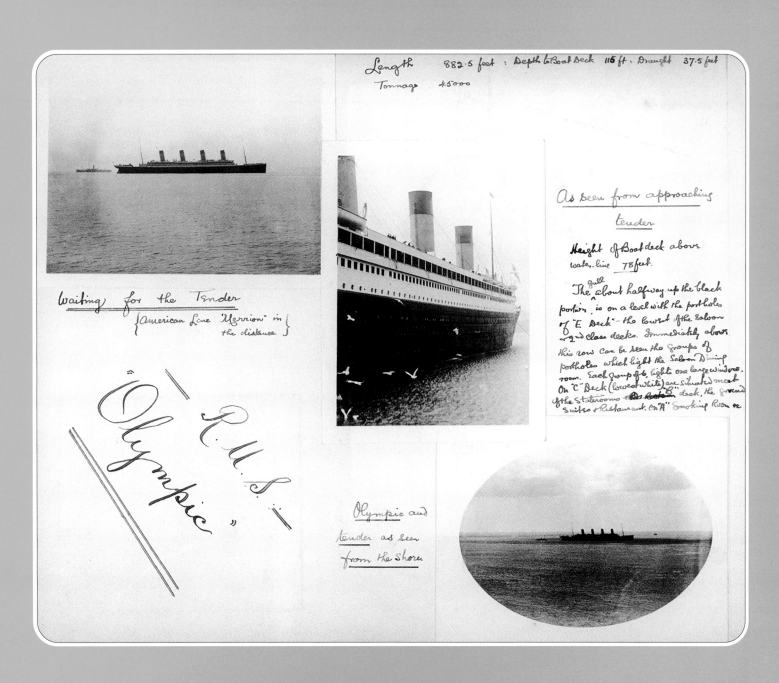

Length 882·5 feet : Depth to Boat Deck 115 ft : Draught 37·5 feet
Tonnage 45000

Waiting for the Tender
{American Line "Merrion" in
the distance}

R.M.S.
"Olympic"

As seen from approaching
tender

Height of Boat deck above
water line 78 feet.

The gull about halfway up the black
portion, is on a level with the port holes
of "E Deck" – the lowest of the Saloon
or 2nd class decks. Immediately above
this row can be seen the groups of
portholes which light the Saloon Dining
room. Each group of 6 light one large window.
On "C" Deck (lowest white) are situated most
of the Staterooms. On "B" deck, the grand
suites & Restaurant. On "A" Smoking Room &c

Olympic and
tender as seen
from the shore.

The Titanic

Sister Ships

The Olympic

"Farewell"

"Berthon" Collapsible on Boat Deck (McL)

The Bridge

These boats open out like
Concertinas: the upper (poled) gunwale
drawing the canvas sides taut, when
the weight of the structure comes
upon them. The wooden floor, seen
folded in the photo goes down, & the
the hinged thwarts straighten out
to form seats. Oars, sails, provisions
&c are seen stored in readiness.

Marconi Room

To replace the Lusitania :—

A Boat with an unlucky name :—

One of the smallest passenger steamers in Transatlantic traffic.

Anchor Line "California"

A forbidden entry

The RMS Lusitania on her outward voyage June 9th 1912 lost one of her propellers. As she was not ready to sail on her next scheduled day — June 20th — the Cunard Co. chartered the Anchor Line "California" to replace her. Very few passengers booked on account of confounding the Anchor Line "California" with the Leyland Line "Californian" whose captain failed to rescue the Titanic passengers.

American Line "Philadelphia" formerly Inman Line "City of Paris"

On the Promenade Deck

An Ocean Greyhound of the Past

Length 576 feet, Beam 63¾ feet
Tonnage 10,800 tons

Shipping the Mails

The last post for a ruined city

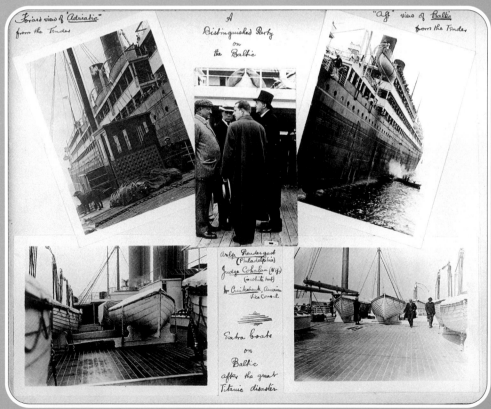

Twin Cunarders — "Franconia" & "Laconia"

"Franconia" passing Roches Point

A glimpse from the tender.

Approaching view

News of the world once more

Passengers eager for News after 10 days at Sea

Landing a large company from the "Franconia"

"Mind your head, Madam". Awkward port of the Franconia

Father Browne's Album

"White Star" Liner of the Olden Time

Length 582 feet
Beam 58 feet

The "Majestic"

Gross tonnage 10,000 t
Horse-power 18,000

Speed 20 knots.

Bringing fresh water to replenish tanks.

Swinging for her course (R.C.)
(Laconia)

The first turn of the propellers

Half - speed

The "Majestic" & her sister-ship the "Teutonic" are not fitted with tanks sufficiently large to supply the lavish fresh water supply demanded by modern travellers, hence

"Bumboats" — Tanks & Tenders

before leaving Queenstown they have to make good the amount used between S'hampton and Queenstown. The tank locally known as "The City of Paris" is towed out, & fresh water supplied. The Majestic was the only Atlantic liner with more than sufficient life boat accomodation before the Titanic disaster.

A Berthon Collapsible Boat under an ordinary life boat.

The last Tender alongside.

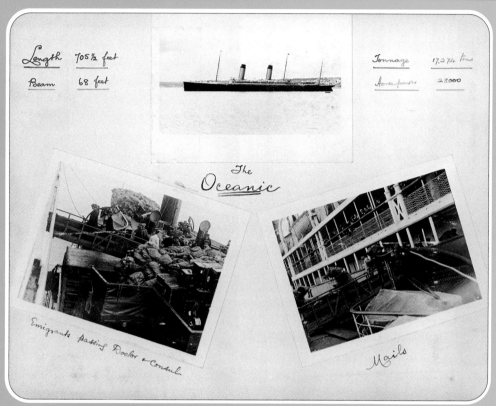

Length 705½ feet
Beam 68 feet

Tonnage 17,274 tons
Horsepower 28000

The *Oceanic*

Emigrants passing Doctor & Consul

Mails

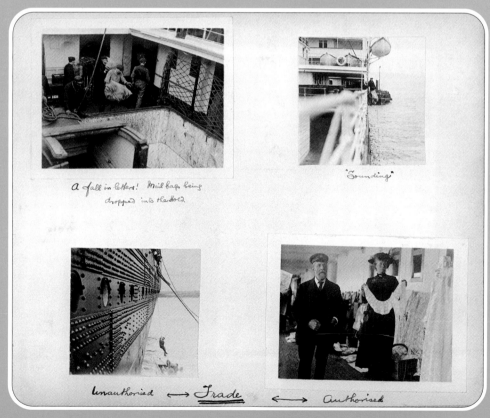

A fall in letters! Mail bags being dropped into the Hold

"Sounding"

Unauthorised ← *Trade* → Authorised

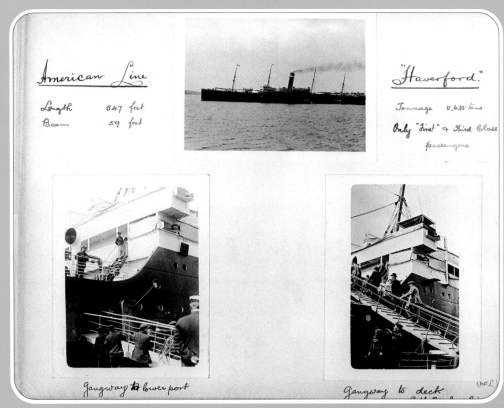

Length 616 ft.
Breadth 56 ft

Tonnage 15,801 tons
Horsepower 10000
Speed 16 knots.

The "Arabic"

Doctor inspecting Eyes
(No passenger suffering from glaucoma or similar diseases is allowed to travel)
(McD)

Stewards transferring baggage.

"Henderson" Collapsible Boats

Rafts — English Style

(After the Titanic Disaster)

Besides the solid gunwales the keels of these boats are also solid. On being lifted up they open like a concertina & are then kept in shape by means of struts & bolts. They can accommodate about 20 people.

Steerage.

These rafts are "self righting" & will float in whatever position they reach the water. They are intended to be thrown overboard in case of accident to be seized by any who may be in the water. In the interior there are long metal cylinders hermetically sealed & containing air, which ensure buoyancy. They are provided with oars & provisions. One of these rafts only sank 2 inches when bearing 20 full grown men.

White Star — Dominion

"Megantic"

Length   565 feet
Beam   65 feet
Tonnage   14,877 tons

Largest vessel trading with Quebec and Montreal

Hoisting the Gangway

Mounting the Gangway

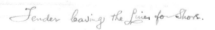

Tender leaving the Liner for Shore.

CLYDE SHIPPING CO.

RETIREMENT OF CAPT. TOBIN

Queenstown, Sunday.

Captain James Tobin, Commodore Captain of the Clyde Shipping Co.'s fleet at Queenstown, has retired after what has been in the fullest sense of the term a strenuous life at sea, and no man could possibly retire from command with a more satisfactory and successful record than to which Captain Tobin can lay claim. He has been over 40 years commanding vessels at Queenstown, and during that period has had many voyages away from...

"Tender Captains"

Captain Tobin — of the "America"

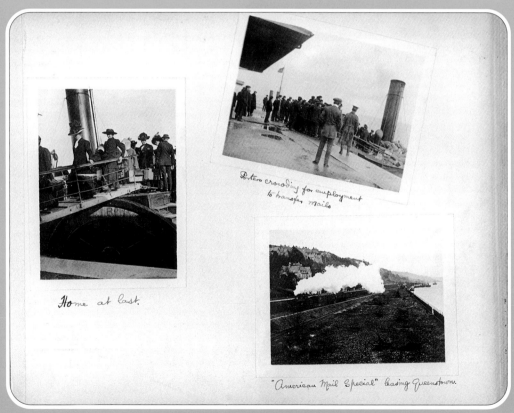

Father Browne's Album

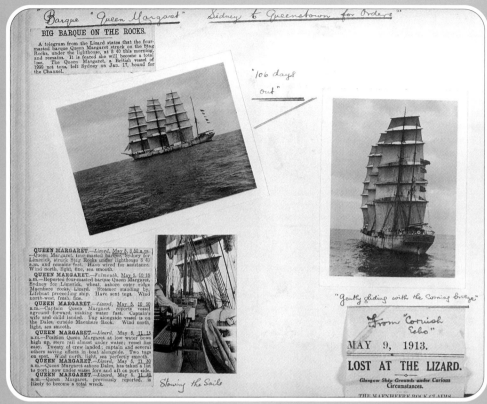

At the Capstan

When Orders Come

Passing the tow-rope to the Tug.

In tow

Stowing the Anchor.

Spreading Sail

A breezy day at Daunt's Rock

The Crew

Of the Tug

"All right aloft?"

Mr A. H. Allen is puzzled.

R.C.Y.C. "Sybil" (w)

"A fair breeze & a flowing Sea"

Names from left :—
Master Jeff Sheehan (nephew of Canon Sheehan)
Mr A. H. Allen (owner of Sybil)
Yachtsman
Mr Davis (secretary to Admiral Coke)
Mr Florence McCarthy
Mr Harold Allen

An
Admiralty
Yacht
of
today

The Enchantress (with Winston Churchill) entering Cork Harbour

and

The arrival of the Port Admiral. (Sir C Staveley Coke)

The "Success" was an old teak built convict ship, built about 1786, & sunk in Sidney Harbour 1831. Raised to the surface & refitted in 1903. She has been leased by a company for show purposes.

This photo was taken in Queenstown on the occasion of her having to put in there to have a damaged mast replaced. She was on her way from L'pool to New York when her Maintop mast got "sprung" about 160 miles west of Queenstown. Summoning aid by "wireless" with which she was fitted, she returned & had the damage made good. She finally left on May 5 arriving in New York about June 30.

a Convict Ship of the Past

2

SHIPS IN PORT

The pictures in this chapter, and those following, have been selected from
the negatives which Father Browne developed between 1921 and 1954.

Below:
*At George's Quay, Dublin (opposite the Custom House) we see the Arklow-built and
Arklow-owned* J. T & S. *discharging cargo into a horse-and-dray.
One of the Guinness ships,* Clarecastle *or* Carrowdore, *is in the background (1944).*

Facing:
Making smoke:
The SS Scotia *en route*
from Wales to Ireland
(1937).

Left:
Children playing on the
mailboat Scotia *en route*
from Holyhead to Dún
Laoghaire, Ireland (1937).

Facing:
Passengers and crew aboard the mailboat
Scotia *await departure from Admiralty Pier,*
Holyhead (1937).

Right:
Two of the London and North Western
Railway Company's steamers – possibly the
Cambria *and the* Hibernia *– at Carlisle Pier,*
Dún Laoghaire, Dublin (1930).

Below:
The Dutch MV Prima *in safe haven, Cork*
(1941). Built in 1931 at Spaarndam, the Prima
weighed 400 gross tons. In 1954 she was sold
to Costa Rican flag operators and in 1955 she
was renamed Bat Galim *by her new Israeli*
owners. She was scrapped in 1968.

Right:
The MV Innisfallen, *taken from the heights above Cobh (1954). This* Innisfallen *should not be confused with her namesake which struck a mine and sank in the River Mersey on 20 December, 1960.*

Below:
Quayside in Cork (1938) with crowds viewing the Finnish sailing-ship Archibald Russell, *a splendid four-masted barque. She was part of the famous Gustaf Erikson fleet of Maarianhamina, Aland, Baltic Sea.*

Left:
British naval vessels – on a courtesy visit to Cork – passing the Belgian training-vessel Mercator *opposite Haulbowline, Cork (1950). The chimneys of Irish Steel Ltd are on the left. The naval provender warehouses in the centre of the picture were constructed for the Royal Navy in the nineteenth century and were among the largest in Europe.*

Below:
The Flower-class corvette, Cliona, *of the Irish naval service passes either the* Irish Plane *or the* Irish Hazel *of Irish Shipping Ltd in front of Haulbowline Island in Cork Harbour (1954).*

Right:
The SS Ardmore *at Cork Harbour (1909). The ship, of 609 gross tons, had been built at Dundee earlier that year. On 13 November, 1917, while sailing from London to Cork, she was sunk in the Irish Sea, with the loss of nineteen souls.*

Below:
SS Seafalke *gets a bashing from the waves at Deepwater Quay, Cobh, Ireland (1934) with her anchor holding her at bay. Two Cork Harbour ferries on the left. Royal Navy ship in background.*

Facing:
Fishermen at Deepwater Quay, Cobh, Ireland. Taken from the Estonian freighter Otto *(1941).*

Left:
Hides for export at Adelphi Quay, Waterford Port (1933).

Below:
The SS Trsat, *registered at Bakar near Fiume, at Limerick Port (1937). This ship was sunk by aircraft on 7 September, 1945.*

Right:

The Greek tramp steamer Antonios Statathos *of Ithaka discharging 6,750 tons of grain at Limerick Port (1937). She was sold to Latvia in 1939 and renamed* Everasma.
On 28 February, 1942, in a position approx. 17°N and 48°W, she was torpedoed and sunk.
Her crew of fifteen were rescued by the Italian submarine Leonardo da Vinci.

Below:

An Irish Sea single-hatch steam coaster, loading pit props for the British coalfields at Wicklow Harbour (1934).

Right:
The wartime fleet, Arklow (1942). To the right of the trawlers is the Arklow-owned schooner Windermere *with her neutral, wartime markings. Built of wood at Connah's Quay, N. Wales, in 1890, she survived until the 1950s.*

Below:
SS Elbe *at Cork Harbour (1933). Dockers stand by, waiting for a call to work.*

3

PEOPLE

The gentleman in the photograph below is Dr Robert Martin of Birkenhead, brother-in-law of the photographer. He is the only person in this chapter who is related to Father Browne. An entire volume could be given to the people he photographed on ships; so what we see here is simply a representative sample.

Emigrant dog (1939). Taken on board the Dublin-Liverpool ferry, MV Munster, *at the North Wall, Dublin. The Irish Lights tender,* Isolda, *is in the background. The* Munster *was built by Harland & Wolff in Belfast for the B&I line. She was mined and sunk in Liverpool Bay on 7 February, 1940. The* Isolda *was built in Dublin and registered at 734 gross tons in 1928. On 19 December, 1940, she sailed from Rosslare with relief-crew members for the Barrels and Coningbeg light vessels. She was attacked and sunk by German aircraft with the loss of six Irish Lights staff with seven others wounded. (The incident was witnessed by the Irish Coastwatching Look-out on Carnsore Point and the crew of the Limerick steamer* Lanahrone.) *Capt. A. Bestic, from Dundrum, Co. Dublin, who was in command of the* Isolda, *was saved. A lucky man, he had also survived the torpedoing of the* Lusitania.

Left:
A little girl admires the wake of SS Scotia en voyage between Holyhead and Dún Laoghaire (1937).

Below:
Passengers aboad the mailboat Scotia await departure for Dún Laoghaire from Admiralty Pier, Holyhead (1937).

Facing:
Look-out from the bridge of the mailboat Scotia (1937): the Second Officer on watch between Wales and Ireland.

Facing:
During the Eucharistic Congress in Dublin (1932), many liners came to visit and were used as hotels. This one was berthed at the Alexandra Basin.

Left:
*The baby arrives!
A Cunard crewman helps a mother disembark from the* Mauretania *with her offspring at Cork Harbour (1938).*

Captain Meskell brings the SS Dún Aengus alongside the pier at Kilronan, Aran Islands (1938).
Beside him on the bridge stands the ship's mate, Michael Folan.

Right:
Over the sea from the Isles: passengers aboard the Islay ferry head for the Scottish port of Kennacraig, near Tarbert (1928).

Below:
The captain of the Jura ferry gives some advice to his helmsman near Port Askaig, Islay, Hebrides (1928).

'The Emigrants' Farewell' at Queenstown (now Cobh) was a traditional custom on the departure of transatlantic liners in the early decades of the 20th century (1934).

4

DISTANT VOYAGES

In January 1924, Father Browne sailed from Falmouth to Australia via Cape Town.
On his return journey at the end of 1925 he sailed from Fremantle to Plymouth
via the Cocos Islands, Ceylon, Suez, Salonica, Naples, Toulon, Gibraltar and Lisbon.
The best of his photographs appeared in *Father Browne's Australia*.

Below:
Panoramic view of Sydney Harbour with ferries plying to and fro (1924).
On the right is the promontory where the foundation-stone
of the famous Harbour Bridge would soon be laid.

Right:
The North Shore ferry Kubu, *Sydney Harbour (1924).*

Below:
The Dutch East Indies liner, the SS Niagara, *getting up smoke at Sydney (1924). A North Shore ferry is moored in the foreground.*

Above:
Streamers fly from SS Houtman *as she prepares to depart from Sydney (1924).*

Right:
Sydney Harbour ferry Parapartoo, *heading towards Circular Quay, Sydney (1925).*

Right:
The pilot's boat, Captain Cook, *near the entrance to Sydney Harbour (1924).*

Below:
Overview of the port, Fremantle (1925), with the SS Mooltan *of Belfast in the foreground. She was built by Harland & Wolff in 1923.*

Facing:
Farewell scene as SS Orama *prepares to depart from the Australian port of Fremantle (1925).*

Facing:
Tug towing SS Orama *along the Brisbane River, Australia (1925).*

Right:
The SS Ferndale *at dock, Cocos Islands, Indian Ocean (1925). Father Browne visited these islands when sailing from Australia to Ceylon (now Sri Lanka) in the autumn of that year.*

Below:
The Yarra River at Williamstown, near Melbourne (1924).

Right:
SS Houson *at port, Cape Town (1924), with Port Authority barge in the foreground.*

Below:
SS Arundel Castle *approaching the docks at Cape Town (1924). Originally built in 1921, the liner was remodelled in 1936 by Harland & Wolff in Belfast with only two funnels and a raked stern.*

Right:
The Union Castle Line's SS Arundel Castle *at Cape Town (1924).*

Below:
SS Arundel Castle *arriving at the dockside, Cape Town (1924).*
During World War II she served as a troopship and also as a 'diplomatically protected repatriation ship'.

Above:
SS Arundel Castle *departing from the quayside, Cape Town (1924). The liner survived until 1959 when she was scrapped in Hong Kong.*

Right:
A calm evening in the port at Cape Town (1924) with Table Mountain in the background. The cable-laying ship SS Canaria *is moored in the foreground.*

Right:
Crewman plumbing the depths off Fremantle breakwater.

Below:
The SS Mooltan *(P&O Line) and ferries at Milson's Point in Sydney Harbour (1924).*
The Mooltan *and her sister ship* Maloja *were the first P&O liners to gross over 20,000 tons.*

The SS Port Melbourne *(1924)*

5

FUN AND GAMES

The journey between Australia and Europe took over a month in the early 1920s, so amusements had to be provided for the passengers. In the days before TV, electronic games and Internet cafés, the diversions were rather simple. This chapter and the lower photograph on page 84 show some of the amusements of the time.

*A canvas awning has been stretched above the promenade deck in preparation
for dancing, fun and games on the SS Orama in the Red Sea (1928).*

Facing:
*Crewman exercising on
SS* Port Melbourne *(1924).*

*Left: In team attire, checking the
noticeboard, SS* Orama *(1925).*

*Below:
Deck tennis aboard the SS* Orama
in the Indian Ocean (1925).

Facing:

*Top left: Deck games aboard the
SS* Orama *in the Indian Ocean (1925).*

*Top right: The egg-and-spoon race on
SS* Orama *en route from Columbo to Aden
(1925).*

Bottom: Gala Day on SS Orama *en route
from Colombo to Aden (1925).*

Right:
Preparing for the Dance: SS Orama *in the
Red Sea (1925).*

Below:
*'Take your Partners' aboard the
SS* Orama *in the Indian Ocean (1925).*

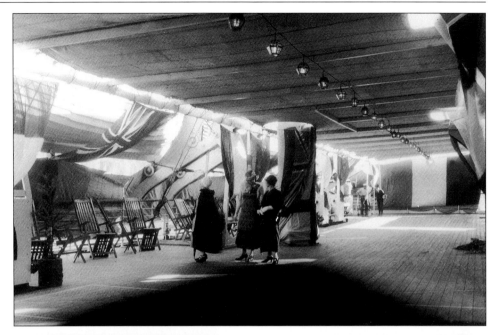

Right:
The local Pipe Band plays for the passengers aboard the Mauretania *during her stop-over in Cork Harbour (1938).*

Below:
'Blind Man's Buff' aboard the SS Orama *in the Indian Ocean (1925).*

6

SHIPPING

Not many passengers on ocean liners have been allowed to bring their cameras below decks, but Father Browne was an exception. He managed to wheedle his way down into the engine-room where, despite the lack of light, he was able to take some of the remarkable pictures shown in this chapter.

London tugboat (1924). The tug is about to tow the Port Melbourne *from the Royal Albert Dock.*

Facing:
*Lighters in the Royal Albert Dock, London (1924).
It was from here that Father Browne set sail, via
Falmouth, for Cape Town and Melbourne.*

Left:
*View from the Mersey ferry, Birkenhead, England
(1939).*

Below:
*The city of Liverpool as seen from a Mersey ferry
(1939).*

Left:
The Swedish sailing-ship C.B. Petersen, *returning from Australia, photographed in Cork Harbour (1930).*

Facing:
Sailors at work in the rigging of the C.B. Petersen, *a Swedish vessel well-known in the 'grain races' from Australia. Photographed off Cobh, County Cork (1930).*

Facing:

Top: Cargo steamers at the South Jetties, Cork (1931), during the great shipping depression. Most of these ships continued trading after 1935, many to fall victim to World War II torpedoes. Both vessels belonged to the Hain Steamship Company, of St Ives, Cornwall.

Bottom: Sir Thomas Lipton's yacht Erin *photographed off Queenstown (now Cobh) in 1904. The millionaire grocer was a keen yachtsman and an intrepid competitor.*

Right:

Harbour dredging at Mornington, Victoria, Australia (1924).

Below:

A view over the stern of a Cork Harbour Commissioners tender on its way to service the Cunard liner Caledonia *in Cork Harbour (1938).*

En route to Australia (1924):
the superstructure of
SS Port Melbourne,
(left) looking forward, and
(right) looking aft.

Facing:

Top: The SS Orama *at Port Said (1925). This ship, on which Father Browne returned from Australia, became a troop-carrier during World War II. The* Orama *was 19,840 gross tons and belonged to the Orient Line. She was sunk on 8 June, 1940, en route from Scapa Flow to Narvik, with the loss of twenty lives.*

Bottom: Screen erected on the promenade deck of SS Orama *in the Indian Ocean (1925). This was probably used for the screening of films in the open air at night – a customary way of entertaining passengers during a long voyage.*

Right:

The motor sounder of SS Orama *(1925). A plumb-line on an extended rod was connected to this motor to record the depth of water beneath the liner's keel.*

Below:

In the shaft-tunnel of SS Orama *(1925): propeller shaft with torsion indicator.*

Facing:
On his return voyage from Australia (1925), Father Browne watched the crew of the Orama *prepare an oceanographic survey cask.*

Right:
The cask is tossed overboard from SS Orama *to measure the Indian Ocean currents between Australia and India (1925).*

Bottom:
In the engine-room of SS Orama *(1925): the triple-expansion turbine engine. The steam turbine was invented by Charles Parsons of Parsonstown (now Birr), County Offaly, Ireland, in 1884.*

Directional wireless on the Dutch tug Humber *at Cobh, Ireland (1930). This was an ultra-modern radio of the time, crucial to the owners of this vessel, Smit & Co., Rotterdam.*

Right:
The tug Ludwig Wiener *(South African Railways & Harbour Administration) at Cape Town (1924).*

Below:
HMS Inflexible *in Cork Harbour (1904). The port remained a major base for the Royal Navy until 1938.*

Right:
The SS Wyreme *embarks a car at Milson's Point, Sydney Harbour (1924).*

Below:
Car-ferry at Middle Harbour, New South Wales (1924).

7

CREW AT WORK

After the *Titanic* tragedy, international law ensured that there was lifeboat space on every ship for everyone aboard. On long voyages, lifeboat drill was carried out scrupulously and the lifeboats were properly maintained – as we can see here. I am reliably informed that many modern ships fall below regulatory standards in this regard.

Lifeboat drill: testing the davits of a lifeboat aboard SS Port Melbourne *during the voyage from Falmouth to Cape Town (1924).*

Facing:
*Lifeboat drill: testing the
McLachlan davits aboard
SS* Port Melbourne *(1924).*

Left:
*'Shooting the sun': crewmen
employing a sextant aboard
SS* Port Melbourne *in the
South Atlantic Ocean (1924).*

Right and below:
*'Shooting the sun': officers employing their sextants aboard
SS* Port Melbourne *in the South Atlantic Ocean (1924).*

Facing:
Desalting the pulleys of lifeboat davits on SS Port Melbourne, *in
the South Atlantic Ocean (1924). Apprentices Braine and Greene
are supervised by Second Officer Newton.*

Facing:
Apprentices Grey and Morgan attending to the paintwork of SS Port Melbourne *as she travels through the Bay of Biscay (1924).*

Left:
The first voyage of Seaman D. Greene (1924). He is pictured here with his mother and aunt on SS Port Melbourne *in the Royal Albert Dock, London. His cap-badge shows the Port Line's house flag.*

Facing:
Captain Kearney of the SS Port Melbourne *in tropical uniform (1924). The inset shows the captain at Falmouth, England, before the voyage to Australia (1924).*

Right:
A hair-cutting session aboard the SS Port Melbourne *(1924). Dr Hawkins supervises the work of Apprentice Morgan on Quartermaster McLeod. Apprentices Worth, Greene and Braine are in attendance.*

Below:
Washing day in the Bay of Biscay (1924). Aboard SS Port Melbourne *are three engineers: T. Little, J. Macpherson and T. Griffiths.*

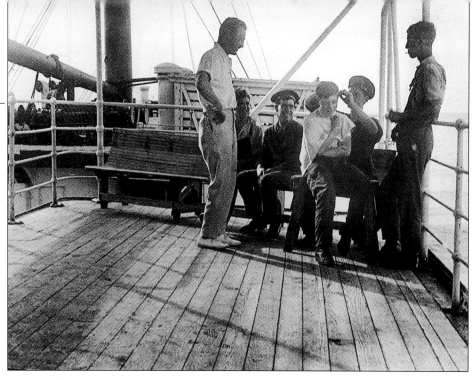

Mr J. McLeod,
Quartermaster,
at the wheel of
SS Port Melbourne
near Cape Town
(1924).

8

SEASCAPES AND SUNSETS

Seascapes form a category of art all on their own; whether in painting or in photography, there is something magical and majestic about them. This final chapter presents several of Father Browne's works which aficionados can contrast with the landscapes presented in previous volumes.

A breezy day in the English Channel off Falmouth. Taken from the deck of SS Port Melbourne *en route for Cape Town (1924). A typical steam coaster can be seen in the distance.*

Right:
A felucca in the Red Sea, photographed from SS Orama *near Port Sudan (1925).*

Below:
Sunset in the Bay of Biscay (1924) as seen from the deck of SS Port Melbourne *on the voyage from England to South Africa.*

Small sea coaster leaving Sligo Port, Ireland (1933).

Right:
The Nogi *(Wales) photographed from*
SS Dún Aengus *shortly after going aground.*
The sailors were rescued by the crew of the
Aran lifeboat, William Evans *(1938).*

Below:
The mailboat Scotia *dispatching mail for the*
Kish Lightship in Dublin Bay (1927).
Note the lifeboat's davits, made to the Welin
patent – as were those of the Titanic.

Left:
Lady Butler admiring an evening view of the Eddystone Lighthouse, 14 miles off Plymouth, England (1925). Father Browne took this picture on the SS Orama *as she was nearing her destination.*

Completed in 1881, this is the fourth lighthouse to stand on the rock, the first having been erected in 1695.

The third lighthouse of 1759, known as 'Smeaton's', had to be dismantled because its foundation was crumbling. It was re-erected on Plymouth Hoe where it still stands as a tourist attraction.

Below:
'The sun goes down on Galway Bay': Father Browne's sunset photo was taken aboard the SS Dún Aengus *en route from Kilronan in the Aran Islands to Galway city (1938).*

APPENDIX

Transcriptions from the Father Browne Album facsimiles. Page numbers refer to the page in this book where the Album facsimile is reproduced. Editor's notes are given in square brackets.

PAGE 17

Top	Emigrants waiting to embark
Bottom left	Passing the Consul and the doctor
Bottom right	'Yanks' and the Detective

PAGE 18

Top left	'Blackthorns and Shamrocks' – Mrs. Galvin
Top right	'All on board the Tenders'
Bottom left	'Waiting to embark'
Bottom right	Last sight of Queenstown

[The tenders in the top right photograph are the *Ireland* and the *America*. In the bottom right picture St Colman's Cathedral can be seen before its spire was erected.]

PAGE 19: UPPER PANEL

Top Left 'In the Offing': *Mauretania*

Length:	790 feet
Breadth	88 feet
Draught (fully loaded)	37½ feet
Depth (Keel–Boat deck)	80 feet
Tonnage	32,000 tons
Height to top of funnels	155 feet
Masts	216 feet
Horsepower	68,000
Speed	25.5 knots
Watertight Compartments	157
Passengers	1st – 550
	2nd – 500
	3rd – 1300
Crew	850

Top right	'At Anchor' – *Mauretania*
Bottom	'The gangway of the *Mauretania*.' Transferring Mails

PAGE 19: LOWER PANEL

Top left 'Emigrants' farewell'

The occasion of this transfer was the arrival from Liverpool by the *Baltic* of some passengers who had missed the slower *Haverford*, and who had been permitted to travel to Queenstown by the *Baltic*. The *Baltic* left Liverpool two hours after the *Haverford* and arrived in Queenstown one and a half hours before her. The tender *Ireland* was returning from the *Baltic* and meeting the *America*, bound to meet the *Haverford*. The passengers and luggage were transferred in the channel.

Centre 'An unusual transfer.'
Tenders changing passengers and baggage in mid-channel.

Bottom right Calm waters near the Harbour's mouth.
Liner (*Celtic*) approaching in the distance.

PAGE 20: UPPER PANEL

MAURETANIA

Top left	The Bridge
Top right	'A' Deck from Bridge, showing extra boats

Capt Sharpe (B of T), Mr Thelwall (P.O.), Mr Dawson (American Vice-Consul). Note 'Chambers' Collapsible Boats. The rear lower portions are solid. The gunwales are of canvas which is kept in position by struts.

Bottom left	Rafts – American Style
Bottom right	Swinging for the Start

PAGE 20: LOWER PANEL

[The bottom three photographs are of the *Lusitania*. The newspaper clipping refers to the death of Mr Tom Martin, Cunard pilot at Queenstown for nearly 30 years. Taken from *Cork Examiner*, 29 November, 1912.]

MAURETANIA

Top left	The Lounge
Top right	The Smoke Room

The Internal decoration alone of the Saloon of the *Mauretania* cost £10,000.

LUSITANIA

Centre	Promenade, with extra boats
Bottom left	'A' Deck
Bottom right	Lounge

PAGE 21

R.M.S. *OLYMPIC*

Top left Waiting for the Tender (American Line *Merrion* in the distance)

Centre

Length	882.5 feet
Depth to Boat Deck	115 feet
Draught	37.5 feet
Tonnage	45,000

As seen from approaching tender.
Height of Boat deck above waterline – 78 feet.
The gull about halfway up the black portion is on a level with the portholes of 'E' Deck – the lowest of the saloon or second class decks. Immediately above this row can be seen the groups of portholes which light the Saloon Dining room. Each group of 6 lights one large window. On 'C' Deck (lowest white) are situated most of the staterooms. On 'B' Deck, the grand suites and restaurant. On 'A' Smoking Room.

Bottom right *Olympic* and tender as seen from the shore

107

PAGE 22: UPPER PANEL

	SISTER SHIPS
Top left	The *Titanic*
Top right	The *Olympic*
Bottom	'Farewell'

[The lower photograph shows the *Olympic* near Crosshaven, County Cork.]

PAGE 22: LOWER PANEL

Top left	'Berthon' Collapsible on Boat Deck.

These boats open out like concertinas: the upper (solid) gunwale drawing the canvas sides taut when the weight of the structure comes upon them. The wooden floor, seen folded in the photo goes down and the hinged thwarts straighten out to form seats.
Oars, sails, provisions etc. are seen stored in readiness.

Top right	The Bridge
Bottom	Marconi Room: Mr Brent

[These pictures are of the *Olympic*, continuing from previous page.]

PAGE 23: UPPER PANEL

To replace the *Lusitania*: a boat with an unlucky name. One of the smallest passanger steamers in Transatlantic Traffic.

Top left	Anchor Line *California*
Top right	A Forbidden Entry
Bottom right	The RMS *Lusitania* on her outward voyage June 9th 1912 lost one of her propellers. As she was not ready to sail on her next scheduled day – June 30th – the Cunard Company chartered the Anchor Line *California* to replace her. Very few passengers booked on account of confounding the Anchor Line *California* with the Leyland Line *Californian*.

[The *Californian* was Captain Lord's infamous liner which was ice-bound on the night of the *Titanic* disaster.]

PAGE 23: LOWER PANEL

An Ocean Greyhound of the Past

Length	576 feet
Beam	63 1/4 feet
Tonnage	10,800

Top left	American Line *Philadelphia* formerly Inman Line *City of Paris*
Top right	On the Promenade Deck
Bottom left	Shipping the Mails
Bottom right	The last post for a ruined city Regina can be read clearly on the mailbag.

[The bottom line, partially missing, explains that the city of Regina, Saskatchewan, Canada, was devastated by a tornado in 1912 with the loss of 28 lives and thousands of dollars of damage.]

PAGE 24: UPPER PANEL

Ocean Twins, 23,700 tons

Top left	The *Adriatic*
Top right	The *Baltic*
Bottom	A stern view – the *Adriatic*

PAGE 24: LOWER PANEL

Top left	Forward view of *Adriatic* from the tender
Top centre	A Distinguished Party on the *Baltic*:

Archbishop Prendergast (Philadelphia)
Judge Cohalan (New York)
Mr Cruickshank, American Vice-Consul

Top right	Aft view of *Baltic* from the Tender
Bottom	Extra boats on *Baltic* after the great *Titanic* disaster

PAGE 25: UPPER PANEL

Twin Cunarders – *Franconia* and *Laconia*

Top left	*Franconia* passing Roches Point
Top right	A glimpse from the tender
Bottom left	Approaching view

PAGE 25: LOWER PANEL

Top centre	News of the World once more Passengers eager for News after 10 days at sea
Bottom left	Landing a large company from the *Franconia*
Bottom right	'Mind your head Madam': awkward port of the *Franconia* and *Laconia*

PAGE 26: UPPER PANEL

Top centre	A White Star liner of the Olden Time: the *Majestic*

Length	582 feet
Beam	58 feet
Gross tonnage	10,000
Horse-power	18,000
Speed	20 knots

Bottom	Bringing fresh water to replenish the tanks

PAGE 26: LOWER PANEL

Top left	Swinging for her course (*Laconia*)
Top right	The first turn of the propellers
Centre	Half-speed

[The captions for the lower photographs seem to read: 'Attention all Gulls' and 'Full speed ahead – *Laconia*'.]

PAGE 27:

Top centre	'Bumboats' – Tanks and Tenders

The *Majestic* and her sister ship the *Teutonic* are not fitted with tanks sufficiently large to supply the lavish fresh water supply demanded by modern travellers, hence before leaving Queenstown they have to make good the amount used between Southampton and Queenstown. The tank locally known as *The City of Paris* is towed out, and fresh water supplied. The *Majestic* was the only Atlantic liner with more than sufficient lifeboat accommodation before the *Titanic* disaster.

Bottom left	A Berthon Collapsible Boat under an ordinary lifeboat
Bottom right	The last Tender along side

PAGE 28: UPPER PANEL

Top centre	The *Oceanic*

Length	705 1/2 feet
Beam	68 feet
Tonnage	17,274 tons
Horsepower	28,000

Bottom left	Emigrants passing Doctor and Consul
Bottom right	Mails

Top left	A fall in letters! Mail bags being dropped into the Hold
Top right	'Sounding'
Bottom left	Unauthorised Trade
Bottom right	Authorised Trade

PAGE 29: UPPER PANEL

Top left	American Line *Haverford*	
	Length	547 feet
	Beam	59 feet
	Tonnage	11,635
	Only 'First' and Third class passengers	
Bottom left	Gangway to lower port	
Bottom right	Gangway to deck	

PAGE 29: LOWER PANEL

Top left	Board of Trade Officials coming in the Launch. When more than one liner has to be cleared the port on any one day, the Board of Trade officials are usually conveyed from one to the other in their own special launch. In this case they are about to board the Tender which was going to the Haverford, after they had 'cleared' the *Baltic*. From right to left: Mr Towers, Mr Dawson (American Vice-Consul) and Capt. Sharpe.
Centre	'Steerage' passengers on *Haverford*.
Bottom right	Sea gulls at rest as seen from deck.

PAGE 30: UPPER PANEL

Top centre	The *Arabic*	
	Length	616 feet
	Breadth	56 feet
	Tonnage	15,801 tons
	Horsepower	10,000
	Speed	16 knots
Bottom left	Doctor inspecting eyes. No passenger suffering from 'glaucoma' or similar diseases is allowed to travel.	
Bottom right	Stewards transferring baggage	
	[By 'glaucoma' above, Father Browne meant trachoma.]	

PAGE 30: LOWER PANEL

Top left	'Henderson' Collapsible Boats. (After the *Titanic* Disaster) Besides the solid gunwales the keels of these boats are also solid. On being lifted up they open like a concertina and are then kept in shape by means of struts and bolts. They can accommodate about 20 people.
Top right	Rafts – English Style These rafts are 'self-righting' and will float in whatever position they reach the water. They are intended to be thrown overboard in case of accident to be seized by any who may be in the water. In the interior there are long internal cylinders thermetically sealed, and containing air, which ensure buoyancy. They are provided with oars and provisions. One of these rafts only sank 2 inches when bearing 20 full-grown men.
Bottom	Steerage

PAGE 31: UPPER PANEL

Top centre	White Star – Dominion, *Megantic*	
	Length	565 feet
	Beam	65 feet
	Tonnage	14,877 tons
	Largest vessel trading with Quebec and Montreal	
Bottom left	Hoisting the Gangway	
Bottom right	Mounting the Gangway	

PAGE 31: LOWER PANEL

Top centre	Tender leaving the Liner for shore
Bottom left	'Tender Captains' Captain Tobin of the America [with his dog, Kelly]
Bottom right	Capt. McVie of the *Ireland* [The newspaper clipping refers to the retirement of Captain Tobin of the tender, *Ireland*. Taken from *Cork Examiner*, 6 January, 1913.]

PAGE 32: UPPER PANEL

Top centre	Harvesters of the Deep
Bottom left	Nearing the Quay
Bottom right	Just in! [The lower left-hand photograph shows a Royal Navy warship, identity uncertain.]

PAGE 32: LOWER PANEL

Top left	Home at Last
Top right	Porters crowding for employment to transfer mails
Bottom right	'American Mail Special' leaving Queenstown

PAGE 33: UPPER PANEL

Top left	Barque *Queen Margaret* Sidney to Queenstown for orders '106 days out'
Top right	'Gently gliding with the evening breeze'
Bottom left	Stowing the Sails [The signal flags of the *Queen Margaret* in the right-hand photograph read: 'N.C.R.D.' The ship was built in Dunbarton in 1893 and registered in Glasgow at 2,144 gross tons. The newspaper clipping refers to the loss of the *Queen Margaret* off the Lizard, Cornwall, 5 – 8 May, 1913. Taken from the *Cornish Echo*, 9 May, 1913.]

PAGE 33: LOWER PANEL

Top left	When Sails are stowed
Top right	'Passing the Rock'
Bottom	Moon's silver path – Cork Head [The Daunt lightship, top right, was painted black like all Irish lightships of the time. In 1954 the process of painting these ships red began. The programme was completed in 1956.]

PAGE 34: UPPER PANEL

Top left	Formalities of the Port. Arrivals of the Customs Officers Inspections by the Board of Trade
Bottom left	'Signal Lamps OK'
Bottom right	Life belts too [Top photograph shows the sailing-ship *Atacama*, registered at Kristiania, now Oslo. 1,147 gross tons, she was built in Liverpool in 1890 and registered there before sale to the Norwegians.]

PAGE 34: LOWER PANEL

	A German Training Ship *Herzogen Cecilie*
Top left	Fresh Provisions
Top right	'On the port tack' off Cape Horn
Centre	The purser and his pets
Bottom left	'Shipping a Sea'
Bottom right	In the Schoolroom

[The Cape Horn photographs were given to Father Browne by a German sailor. The caption of the final photograph is almost missing in the original but reads: 'In the Schoolroom'. The *Herzogen Cecilie* was eventually acquired by the Scandinavian ship-owner, Gustaf Erikson.]

PAGE 35: UPPER PANEL

	When Orders Come
Top left	At the Capstan
Top right	Passing the tow-rope to the Tug
Bottom	In tow: stowing the Anchor

[The photographs on this page are of the sailing-ship *Sylfid*. 1,545 gross tons, she was built in Southampton in 1884. First registered at Rauma, Finland, she later sailed under the Russian flag.]

PAGE 35: LOWER PANEL

Top left	Spreading Sail
Top right	A breezy day at Daunt's Rock
Bottom	The Crew of the Tug

[Daunt's Rock lightship, top right, drifted from her moorings on 13 February, 1936. Her crew of eight were rescued in rough weather by the Ballycotton lifeboat, County Cork. The lifeboatmen won the only Gold Medal ever awarded in Ireland.]

PAGE 36: UPPER PANEL

Top left	'All right aloft?' Mr A.H. Allen is puzzled
Top centre	R.C.Y.C. *Sybil*
Top right	'A Fair breeze and a flowing Sea'

Names from left:
Master Jeff Sheehan (nephew of Canon Sheehan),
Mr A.H. Allen (Owner of *Sybil*),
Mr Davies (Secretary to Admiral Coke),
Mr Florence McCarthy, Mr Harold Allen

[The letters 'R.C.Y.C.' stand for the Royal Cork Yacht Club, the oldest yacht club in the world.
The 'Canon Sheehan' mentioned in the right-hand caption was an Irish novelist.]

PAGE 36: LOWER PANEL

	An Admiralty Yacht of Today and a Convict Ship of the Past
Top left	The *Enchantress* (with Winston Churchill) entering Cork Harbour
Top right	The arrival of the port admiral (Sir C. Stanley Coke)
Bottom	The *Success* was an old teak-built convict ship, built about 1786, and sunk in Sidney Harbour 1831. Raised to the surface and refitted in 1903, she has been leased by a company for show purposes. This photo was taken in Queenstown on the occasion of her having to put in there to have a damaged mast replaced. She was on her way from Liverpool to New York when the maintop mast got 'sprung' about 160 miles west of Queenstown. Summoning aid by 'wireless' with which she was fitted she returned and had the damage made good. She finally left on May 5th arriving in New York about June 30th.

INDEX